Money Is No

CW00383683

Why Society Can Afford
Everything it Needs to Thrive

Dean Robertson

How we create money from nothing and can use this
power to tackle our biggest issues.

ASIN: B0BFPHP5WZ

ISBN: 9798353594697

For Freya and Victoria, the source of my happiness and my inspiration to make the world a more abundant and safe place.

"The first lesson of economics is scarcity: there is never enough of anything to fully satisfy all those who want it. The first lesson of politics is to disregard the first lesson of economics."

Thomas Sowell, American author

Contents

Introduction

"Our problems are manmade. Therefore, they can be solved by man. And man can be as big as he wants. No problem of human destiny is beyond human beings."

John F Kennedy, US President

At the time of writing in late summer 2022, you'd be forgiven for not feeling hopeful about the future of humanity. We are facing multiple interconnected crises - cost of living, climate, healthcare and wellbeing. Even freedom and relative world peace is under threat in a way not seen since the Second World War. Each person has their own unique views and priorities on tackling the significant issues facing the global community. This diversity of opinion and the scale of the challenges are daunting. However, nothing is beyond us and there are numerous solutions available if we can come together to utilise our talents, technology and resources effectively.

What often prevents us from doing this is finance and the associated politics that go with it. There are plenty of things we could spend money on - infrastructure, healthcare, defence, social care, green energy, education, the natural environment and a myriad of others. Expenditure on these would benefit people across society and help alleviate threats we face. However, we're often told that we don't have enough money available or that we need to defund something to provide something else. We frequently argue that 'someone else' should pay.

This book aims to demonstrate that *society can afford to tackle all our issues* without creating rampant inflation or raising taxes significantly, either now or for future generations. Indeed, we can even use government and private expenditure to reduce inflation, instead of just accepting the economic hardship caused by raising interest rates.

The cost of inaction and inadequate investment in people, the environment and the economy are significantly greater and even threaten the existence of civilised society itself. Doing much needed investments across our communities and the environment should create a virtuous cycle that increases economic growth, raises tax revenues and expands the pool of wealth that can finance government and private expenditure indefinitely.

Specifically, this book will:

- Explain what money is and how it is created in modern economies.

- Explain what inflation is and how it is measured and controlled.

- Explain what government (public / national) debt really is.

- Demonstrate how society's priorities and needs can be funded without causing inflation and without raising taxes now or in the future.

- Show that the decision not to fund something with government money is *always* a political choice and not born out of necessity.

- Argue that it's possible to stimulate sustainable high economic growth so that society is happy, healthy and prosperous in perpetuity.

- Suggest what each of us can do to bring about a better future for all.

The key to society thriving is the creation of money and its investment in key priorities in a non-inflationary way, as well as growing the real productive capacity of the economy - people's skills, technology, manufacturing and the ecosystem services provided by our natural environment. As will be explained, the creation of money is something both the public and private sector does and both will need to work together to tackle the significant issues we are all facing. This is the promise and potential of something called Modern Monetary Theory (MMT), which I believe describes the realities of our financial system better than any other theory to date.[1]

This book is intended to be neutral politically, ambivalent to what exactly each country chooses to invest in and the balance between the private and public sectors. It is written from a UK economist's perspective and largely uses the UK as an example when exploring economic concepts. However, the ideas discussed are applicable internationally and several great works that have informed this book are from outside the UK.

In particular, the excellent book, *The Deficit Myth: Modern Monetary Theory and How to Build a Better Economy* by Professor Stephanie Kelton, started me off on my journey of awakening to the reality of our economic system in an accessible way. I wish to raise awareness of her and MMT's messages further and link them to other concepts and ideas which could improve our collective prosperity and sustainability. Her book is written largely from a US perspective, as are most books on this topic, and I want to show that the ideas are also applicable in the UK, Europe and elsewhere. In addition, I hope to demonstrate that MMT implies a significant role for individuals and the private sector in unlocking the power of finance for the greater good.

The theory argues that size of government deficits and debts don't matter and taxation isn't needed to fund public expenditure (but is still important). The real limit to what can be spent is the real productive resources of the economy and inflation.[2] This is something that should be widely understood and acknowledged by politicians and the public when making policy decisions or when discussing whether we can afford to do something or not.

I hope that by the end of the book you will have a new perspective on public debt, how money is created and how its power can be harnessed to bring about positive change for society. Our freedom and quality of life and those of our children and grandchildren are at stake, and we are running out of time to leave them holistically better off than us in a sustainable way.

At the time of writing just ahead of the northern hemisphere winter 2022/23, many in both the richer and poorer parts of the world are facing significant hardship due to the cost of living crisis. Lives are literally at stake as people could die from illnesses caused by insufficient nutrition and heating of homes, as individuals can't afford to properly eat and pay their soaring energy bills. There is both a need to ensure that households have sufficient financial support to get them through the emergency situation we are facing this winter and to ensure that investments are made to alleviate the fundamental and long term issues that have caused this crisis (discussed later).

The government cannot do this alone. The success of our human endeavour depends on the public sector, private organisations and individuals all working together and using all the available financial tools at our disposal responsibly. I hope that by reading this book you feel more optimistic about our collective prospects and inspired that something can be done to materially improve our lives over time, by taking actions and investments now. We can and do deserve better than what our current system is delivering and must become the responsible stewards of our precious and unique planet that we have the potential to be.

As will be covered in the following chapters, currency can be created digitally without limit by all of us and this power should be used responsibly to enhance real prosperity. I hope you will see the truth that *money is no object and society can afford everything it needs to thrive*.

Introduction References

[1] Modern Monetary Theory is a term first coined by Australian economist Bill Mitchell, Lockert, 2022 (Business Insider)

[2] The Deficit Myth: Modern Monetary Theory and How to Build a Better Economy, Kelton, 2020 (John Murray Publishers Ltd)

Note from the Author

Thank you for taking the time to read this book and I hope you enjoy it. If you find it interesting and worthy of wider readership, I would be extremely grateful if you could please leave a review on the Kindle / Amazon Store and share, as it helps it reach more people.

All views expressed and any shortcomings in understanding or explanation are mine alone. I would like to thank my talented wife Victoria for her diligent proofreading and clarity suggestions, and for designing the front cover.

Feel free to reach out to me on Twitter - @dean_econ - to discuss the book.

Thanks,

Dean

1. How money is created in modern economies

"It is well enough that people of the nation do not understand our banking and monetary system, for if they did, I believe there would be a revolution before tomorrow morning."

Henry Ford, American Industrialist

Key Points

- **Money is a medium of exchange, a unit of account and a store of value over time.**

- **It has no intrinsic value.**

- **It derives its value from its use, people's trust in it and its legal status.**

- **The vast majority of money is digital and stored in computers.**

- **It is created when loans are issued, so all money is debt.**

- **When debt is repaid, money is destroyed; apart from any residual interest collected by commercial issuers of loans.**

- **There is no hard limit to how much money could be created.**

- **Interest can be thought of as the price of or a tax on money.**

We take money for granted (even if it often feels like it's hard to come by!) and we think we understand it as we use it so often. When asked about it, most people mention notes and coins, the balance in your bank account and the income you earn or are given from others. While this is what we see and experience every day, the majority of individuals (economists included!) don't really understand what money is or how it is created.

Money is a medium of exchange and it has been around in one form or another for thousands of years. Without it, people would have to barter and you would have to go through the effort of finding someone who, for example, wants your fish and is willing to exchange it for their loaf of bread.[1]

It is much more efficient to have a currency that is widely accepted and which allows trading through time - e.g. you can catch and sell your fish in spring and buy your bread in autumn after the harvest. Quite simply, modern society wouldn't have evolved without it, as civilisation relies on specialisation and trade and this is significantly more difficult with a barter economy. Money also measures the prices of things and lets you compare the market cost of many goods and services on a consistent basis. It is a store of value as well, as it allows you to save for purchases needed in the future.[1]

As recently as 1971, the major currencies of the world could theoretically be exchanged for a fixed amount of gold due to the Bretton Woods System. Following World War Two, the dollar became the global reserve currency as the US was the only country with enough wealth to fund the reconstruction of the economies devastated by the war. The Western European, Canadian, Japanese and Australian nations fixed their currencies' exchange rates against the dollar and the US agreed to hold sufficient gold to swap dollars for it if requested.[2]

While this helped stabilise finances and trade between those nations for reconstruction, the system gradually became unworkable due to the gold reserve requirement, the ability to maintain fixed exchange rates and a breakdown of trust that there was sufficient gold available to honour the agreement. In 1971, President Nixon abandoned the gold standard of the dollar and therefore all the currencies pegged to it.[2]

As a result, the majority of the world's currencies lost their intrinsic value virtually overnight and became what is known as fiat currencies. Their value is now solely derived from their continued use and people's trust that they will continue to be accepted by others now and in the future. This is supported by the legal status of sovereign money, which dictates that all taxes must be paid in the currency of a country (or an area like the Eurozone) and only the central bank can commission new notes and coins.[3]

While this gives governments a monopoly over the currency in use in a particular jurisdiction, it doesn't mean that they or the central bank have full control over the creation or amount of money in circulation. As an aside, it should be noted that there are examples of independent local currencies and there is the recent rise of cryptocurrencies to move away from government backed money. However, these are not the focus of this book and not necessarily contradictory to its key messages.

According to the Bank of England[4] (BoE - the UK's central bank), just 3% of all currency in circulation is physical notes and coins. This means that 97% of money is simply digits in computers, and this ratio is similar across the advanced economies of the world. Of this, 18% is central bank reserves (discussed later) and 79% is bank deposits of individuals, businesses and other organisations including those in the public sector. So where does this digital currency, which makes up the overwhelming majority of all money in existence, actually come from?

There are three types of money in the UK economy

3% Notes and coins 18% Reserves 79% Bank deposits

Source: Bank of England[5]

Well, the answer is it is simply created by commercial banks when they make loans! This is worth pausing over and considering further. In their 2014 paper, the BoE make a point of saying from the outset: *"the central bank does not fix the amount of money in circulation, nor is central bank money 'multiplied up' into more loans and deposits"* and that *"[commercial] bank lending creates deposits"*, not the other way round.[4] Intuitively, people think that you put your money in a bank or the central bank creates money which they give to financial institutions, who then loan it out with interest.

Indeed, you may have heard of Fractional Reserve Banking where commercial banks are required to keep so much capital from deposits, say 10%, and can loan out the remaining 90%. This remaining 90% becomes a deposit at another bank or even in the same bank and 90% of that can be loaned out and so on. If the original deposit was £1,000, just £100 would be needed to be retained by the bank and, in theory, that original £100 could be underpinning multiple loans to a value many times more than the total original £1,000 deposit![6]

However, even this rather weak limitation to the money supply doesn't exist in practice according to BoE and economists such as Professor Richard Werner.[7] Banks can and do create money out of nothing when they issue loans through strokes of a keyboard and the creation and crediting of customer accounts. No direct interaction is needed with any money in anyone else's account, another bank or the central bank and no money moves from elsewhere.

Commercial banks don't actually need to check if they have enough deposits to do the lending as they can balance their liquidity later with the central bank. Through the act of issuing a loan, a new liability is created for the person or organisation doing the borrowing and an equally valued asset is created for the bank issuing the loan. This money didn't exist anywhere previously and now it does!

The below graph from Positive Money[8], an organisation which advocates for reforms to create a fair, democratic, and sustainable banking system, shows how the digital money supply in the UK has significantly increased since 1970 relative to notes and coins. This demonstrates the power of the financial system to create currency and how digital commercial bank money has grown to significantly outstrip hard currency.

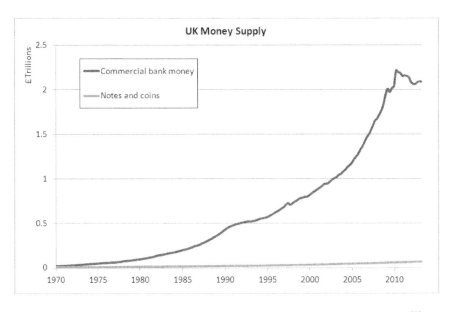

Source: Positive Money[9]

Commercial banks do interact with the central bank through central bank reserves and the interest rate (price) they set on those reserves.[10] Central bank reserves are accounts that banks hold with the monetary authority akin to a current account. They ensure that commercial financial institutions can meet the withdrawal requirements of customers and liquidity and financial stability criteria, which underpin confidence in the banking system.[11]

However, those reserves are provided on demand and created from nothing by the central bank. If a commercial bank has loaned out (created) more money than it needs to meet requirements, it can obtain the reserves from other banks. If that isn't possible, the central bank will simply create those reserves as needed so the system meets requirements.

The commercial bank pays interest on those reserves at a rate set by the central bank, which also determines the charges between financial institutions when they lend to each other. They can choose to pay them down or transfer them to other banks if they are no longer required. This avoids unnecessary interest payments that eat into profits. The BoE and other central banks essentially provide an open promise to the financial system to create reserves as needed and to act as the lender of last resort in their country. Therefore, commercial banks have no incentive to hold surplus reserves unless they have to and because they can always obtain more as needed to meet liquidity requirements.[11]

The conclusion from the above is that all money *is* created from debt and therefore is debt. You may find this disconcerting. As individuals or businesses, debt is often seen as a bad thing that is expensive and something which can cripple your finances. In truth, debt is neither good nor bad in and of itself, just as money is neither good nor bad (they are the same thing, remember!). What matters is what it is used for and whether it can be paid off by income received from valued activities in society.

One interesting implication of money being created from loans is that when you pay off debts you destroy money![5] It is removed from circulation and no longer exists. It reduces the value of your liability but it also reduces the value of the equivalent asset of the debt issuer. Again, this isn't a bad or good thing in and of itself, but it's sobering to know that all the money that disappears from your account each month on mortgages, loans and credit cards also disappears from existence altogether! The same applies to commercial banks when they pay down reserves they no longer require with the central bank or pay interest on those reserves.

However, any interest you pay on private debts is the residual profit that is now available to the bank to cover expenses, pay shareholders and invest in other profit generating assets. Any interest you receive for savings is your profit for lending your money to the bank via your account and reducing the need for them to have interest charging central bank reserves (the liquidity constraint is deposits + reserves, with the latter flexing as needed). This means that interest rates are extremely important and influential on the money supply and wider economy. They are in effect the price of creating and using money and can be thought of as a tax on money.[10]

Unfortunately, they are a particularly regressive form of taxation as the richest in society often pay the lowest interest rate for credit, due to them being considered less risky and having assets to use as collateral. When a bank decides if they will issue a loan (create money) and for how much interest, they will consider how likely it is to be repaid and for them to therefore make a profit. They will consider the income of the applicant and how safe it is, their track record of paying previous debts and any assets, such as houses, to be included as collateral that could be seized and sold as part of the agreement if the loan isn't repaid.[12]

The more safe and attractive you appear as a borrower or the more sound your proposition seems if you are a business, the lower interest you will pay on debt. This is because it is assumed you are lower risk, more likely to pay and the bank is therefore more likely to make a return from you. You are also more likely to have a larger number of available lenders seeking your business and so that competition also drives down the price (interest rate) you are quoted.

At the other end of the spectrum is someone or an organisation with low or no income, a bad record of servicing debt, no assets and probably few available sources of credit. They are likely to be either refused the loan or quoted a higher interest rate (price) for the issuer to take on the risk of you not repaying. While this is reasonable and logical from the point of the view of the bank, it does mean the poorest in society struggle to create money for businesses and can face higher housing or other repayment costs for any debt accrued.

The central bank interest rate effectively creates a floor or baseline for the interest rate commercial banks can charge individuals and organisations for credit, as it puts a constraint on what they need to recoup in interest to remain profitable. In theory, banks could charge loan rates less than the BoE base rate or pay interest on savings at a greater rate, but this means they would be making a loss on those loans and deposits. Therefore, they tend to adjust the price of money with the base rate (and charge a healthy mark-up on top!). Banks also lend to each other and so increasing the central bank interest rate also increases their borrowing costs, which need to be recovered from their customers.

Just as with individuals and non-financial organisations, when commercial banks pay interest on or pay off their reserves with the central bank, the money is simply destroyed. The central bank has no need for an account as the base source of money in the economy. It can simply create any reserves needed in the future with some keystrokes just as easily as it can destroy them, and so has no reason to have its own overarching 'central reserve current account' with deposits and withdrawals. However, it does have a balance sheet with total liabilities such as central bank reserves held by commercial banks and assets such as government bonds owned, which are discussed later.[11]

To recap:

- **Money is a medium of exchange, a unit of account and a store of value over time.**

- **It has no intrinsic value.**

- **It derives its value from its use, people's trust in it and its legal status.**

- **The vast majority of money is digital and stored in computers.**

- **It is created when loans are issued, so all money is debt.**

- When debt is repaid, money is destroyed; apart from any residual interest collected by commercial issuers of loans.

- There is no hard limit to how much money could be created.

- Interest can be thought of as the price of or a tax on money.

Chapter 1 References

[1] The History of Money, Beattie, 2022 (Investopedia)

[2] Cooperation and reconstruction (1944–71) (International Monetary Fund)

[3] Scope of monetary policy (European Central Bank)

[4] Money creation in the modern economy, McLeay et al., 2014 (Bank of England)

[5] How is money created?, 2019 (Bank of England)

[6] Fractional Reserve Banking, Kagan 2022 (Investopedia)

[7] How do banks create money, and why can other firms not do the same? An explanation for the coexistence of lending and deposit-taking, Werner, 2014 (Science Direct)

[8] Our Vision (Positive Money)

[9] UK Money Supply, Jackson (Positive Money)

[10] How Central Banks Create Money, Ryan-Collins et al. (Positive Money)

[11] Understanding the central bank balance sheet, Rule, 2015 (Bank of England)

[12] Banks Are Giving the Ultra-Rich Cheap Loans to Fund Their Lifestyle, Pendleton & Stupples, 2021 (Bloomberg)

2. What is inflation, how is it measured and how is it controlled?

"Inflation is as violent as a mugger, as frightening as an armed robber and as deadly as a hit man. Inflation is taxation without legislation. The first panacea for a mismanaged nation is inflation of the currency; the second is war. Both bring a temporary prosperity; both bring a permanent ruin."

Ronald Reagan, US President

Key Points

- **Inflation is the general increase in the price of goods and services over time.**

- **It represents a devaluation of money and a loss in its purchasing power.**

- **Inflation is an estimated statistical construct that has its limitations and there are different types of indices.**

- Regional and personal inflation can be significantly different from national inflation.

- The central bank's primary remit is to keep inflation low and stable (typically a 2% target).

- The primary way in which inflation is controlled is via interest rates set by the central bank.

- An increase in interest rates normally lowers inflation as it makes the cost of money (debt) higher, reduces the cost of imports and can lead to higher unemployment, which reduce demand for goods and services.

- Central banks are normally independent from the government to give inflation targets credibility and to avoid politicians 'bribing' people near elections with low interest rates.

Intrinsically linked to the creation of money is the concept of inflation. Inflation is a general rise in the prices of goods and services over a given period or equivalently a fall in the purchasing power of a currency (a devaluation).[1] There is also deflation, which is the opposite case - a general fall in the prices of economic outputs and a consequent rise in the purchasing power of money.

High inflation will erode the real purchasing power of people over time when incomes do not keep up with the cost of living. This can stop economic growth as people cut back on consumption or take on increasingly costly debt. Deflation is also considered undesirable as it encourages people to hold off spending in anticipation of lower prices in the future and this can also lead to a collapse in economic output in a self-reinforcing cycle.

Low and stable inflation is generally the goal of central banks across the world, with most countries targeting around 2% annually to ensure people keep spending.[2] This means that real purchasing power is (hopefully!) at least maintained by rising incomes. In practice this means that if a family's groceries, utilities and entertainment cost £1,000 per month this year, they should cost £1,020 next year if inflation is on target. As long as the household income increases by at least 2%, then they should be no worse off in real terms. If their income stays the same or falls then they will have to reduce the quantity or quality of things they purchase or take on more debt to keep consumption the same.

At the time of writing in August 2022, UK annual inflation as measured by the Consumer Price Index (CPI - more on this later) is at more than 10%[3], with some forecasts predicting it will rise close to 20% in 2023.[4] A rate as high as this hasn't been seen since 1990 and is largely driven by the supply chain impacts of geopolitical events (Russia's invasion of Ukraine) and the aftermath of the Covid pandemic. Other economies around the world are facing similar rates of inflation that are much higher than recent history. This means that the cost of living is facing significantly more attention in the headline news than is typical. Incomes are simply not keeping pace with the rate of price increases, so the real purchasing power of households is falling significantly and a widespread recession is considered highly likely in late 2022 / early 2023.[5]

The upcoming winter in the northern hemisphere is predicted to be extremely hard for many families all over the world, with those even in rich countries facing a choice between heating and eating. It's no exaggeration to say there are likely to be excess and preventable winter deaths, unless comprehensive support is given to the most vulnerable. The graph below from the Office of National Statistics shows how UK inflation has accelerated in the past year from previously being around the 2% target for the previous decade.[6]

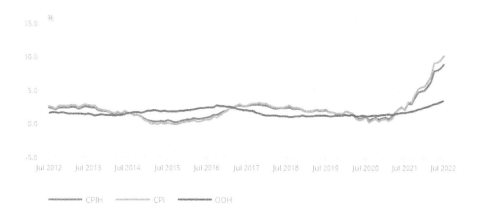

Figure 1: Annual CPIH inflation rate highest since December 1990

CPIH, OOH component and CPI annual inflation rates for the last 10 years, UK, July 2012 to July 2022

Source: Office for National Statistics[6]

Inflation is a statistical construct and it is worth exploring how it is measured and what is and isn't included. The UK statistical authority, the Office of National Statistics, is in charge of producing monthly inflation figures and compiling the various indices used in the UK. They use a sampling approach of a representative basket of goods and services to derive the figures and weight elements according to their influence on households' costs.[7] While the ONS follows international standards of rigour in compiling these statistics, there are significant challenges in compiling a single annual inflation figure for an entire nation that is both accurate and representative.

The preferred measure of inflation by ONS is Consumer Price Index including Housing (CPIH) as this includes Owner Occupier Costs incurred by British households (such as rent, mortgage repayments and home maintenance). This is considered more reflective of the cost of living than just the Consumer Price Index or Retail Price Index (an older measure of inflation still linked to certain UK contracts such as phone bills), which include just goods and services. The ONS website contains significant detail and articles on inflation, how it is measured and plans for improving the measurement of inflation over time. [7]

While the ONS is required to produce national inflation figures monthly, the inflation rates of different parts of the UK can differ significantly as measured by CPIH. For example, the housing market in London could be booming and is likely to be a greater proportion of household costs due to high mortgage and rental values. Whereas a rural community in Wales or on an island off the coast of Scotland may have stagnant or even falling house prices, which may already be relatively cheap compared to local incomes. In those locations, residents are likely to have much higher transport and heating costs due to their remoteness, meaning the cost of fuel and energy has a much bigger impact on their overall expenditure.

Even within the same region, individuals and households could face very different personal inflation rates due to their circumstances. For example, a particular household may have access to only one supermarket due to transport or mobility limitations. That shop could be raising prices at a much different rate than the rest of the market and could be significantly different in prices to the average shop to start with. UK Campaigner Jack Monroe has recently convinced the ONS to release inflation statistics for different socio-economic groupings, such as those on low incomes, to show how inflation affects different parts of society, and especially the poorest.[8] This work is to be commended and there are now various tools available to calculate your personal inflation rate.

Despite different individuals facing very different rates of inflation at any given time, for practical reasons the Bank of England target applies only to national CPI (and not CPIH). This is because the main lever the central bank uses to control inflation to try and keep it on target is by setting interest rates. As discussed previously, interest rates have a significant impact on the money supply and economy because it is the price of money, and therefore the cost of debt.[9]

A higher interest rate means that households with a mortgage on a variable rate immediately start paying higher amounts on their mortgage repayments. Even households on fixed rates for certain periods face the market rate when they expire, and so are exposed to higher interest rates and therefore repayment costs eventually. In addition, the expectation of facing higher costs in the near future is likely to cause households to cut back on spending now.[10]

Renters are also more likely to face higher costs as their landlords are facing higher repayment costs on their investment mortgages, which they pass on to tenants. Other forms of loans and credit can also be linked to the central bank rate and so non-housing personal loans and credit increase in cost too, along with the price of any new borrowing taken on. All of this extra expenditure on servicing debt reduces the amount available to spend on goods and services and the idea is that price rises will slow due to the resulting drop in demand.

An increase in interest rates will normally also attract international money seeking a higher return and push up the value of a currency compared to trading partners. This will reduce import costs as, for example, your same quantity of pounds can now buy more goods produced in the Eurozone. Advanced economies such as the UK typically import more goods and services than they export, so a rise in the value of the pound will also likely reduce inflation.[11]

Increasing interest rates also increases the costs of borrowing for businesses and organisations, as well as the costs of labour due to pay rises that are often linked to inflation. Therefore, it can lead to businesses laying off workers and unemployment increasing, which further reduces consumption demand in the economy. Therefore, the price of controlling inflation is often pain and hardship for many and a reversal of economic growth if done via interest rates. It need not be this way, as is discussed later.[12]

The reason the BoE doesn't have a target based on CPIH is that by raising the interest rate they raise the H (housing costs) element of the index. It would be impractical for them to have an inflation target based on an index that increases each time they increase rates, as the purpose of doing so is to bring inflation down! In truth, what the central bank is doing is attempting to shift the inflation of goods and services to the cost of money to bring demand and supply of goods and services back into balance.

The 2% CPI (or equivalent internationally) inflation target that is widely adopted by the major global economies isn't set in stone, and indeed appears to be a rather arbitrary figure that is widely credited to the Governor of the Reserve Bank of New Zealand in 1988.[13] There is no evidence-based reason why the target couldn't be slightly higher or lower, but it is generally agreed that a low and positive inflation target is best.

One final thing to say on central banks and inflation targets is that in recent decades there has been a consensus that central banks should be independent from political interference.[14] This is because politicians may be tempted to lower interest rates to 'bribe' people to vote for them in the run up to elections by making them temporarily feel richer. There is a lag between interest rate changes and prices changes, so it is possible to lower interest rates and for people to have more cash available for goods and services before the prices increase to account for the newly created higher demand.

The BoE and other major central banks are mostly officially independent and are primarily concerned with controlling inflation. It gives the target more credibility and raises expectations that it will be met, which matters when influencing people's and organisation's behaviour. However, governments are involved in the appointment of officials to the monetary authorities, so there is always scope for influence. They do also have secondary remits to maintain economic stability and growth, which means the setting of interest rates to control inflation is always a balancing act and political in nature.

To recap:

- **Inflation is the general increase in the price of goods and services over time.**

- It represents a devaluation of money and a loss in its purchasing power.

- Inflation is an estimated statistical construct that has its limitations and there are different types of indices.

- Regional and personal inflation can be significantly different from national inflation.

- The central bank's primary remit is to keep inflation low and stable (typically a 2% target).

- The primary way in which inflation is controlled is via interest rates set by the central bank.

- An increase in interest rates normally lowers inflation as it makes the cost of money (debt) higher, reduces the cost of imports and can lead to higher unemployment, which reduce demand for goods and services.

- Central banks are normally independent from the government to give inflation targets credibility and to avoid politicians 'bribing' people near elections with low interest rates.

Chapter 2 References

[1] Inflation: Prices on the Rise, Oner (International Monetary Fund)

[2] Inflation and the 2% target (Bank of England)

[3] Consumer price inflation, UK: July 2022 (Office of National Statistics)

[4] The U.K. could see almost 20% inflation by January, according to Citigroup, Daniel, 2022 (Fortune)

[5] Global economy: Outlook worsens as global recession looms - IMF (United Nations)

[6] Consumer price inflation, UK: July 2022 (Office of National Statistics)

[7] Inflation and price indices (Office of National Statistics)

[8] Cost-of-living crisis: Jack Monroe hails ONS update of inflation calculations, Elliot, 2022 (Guardian)

[9] Scope of monetary policy (European Central Bank)

[10] Why have interest rates gone up? (Bank of England)

[11] How National Interest Rates Affect Currency Values and Exchange Rates, Lioudis, 2022 (Investopedia)

[12] What Is the Relationship Between Inflation and Interest Rates?, Folger, 2022 (Investopedia)

[13] The Fed's inflation target comes from a casual remark on New Zealand TV, Subramanian, 2021 (Quartz)

[14] What Has Central Bank Independence Ever Done for Us?, Haldane, 2020 (Bank of England)

3. What is government (public / national) debt and does it matter?

"Let us never forget this fundamental truth: the State has no source of money other than money which people earn themselves. If the State wishes to spend more it can do so only by borrowing your savings or by taxing you more. It is no good thinking that someone else will pay – that 'someone else' is you. There is no such thing as public money; there is only taxpayers' money."

Margaret Thatcher, UK Prime Minister

Key Points

- **Public debt represents a liability for the government that must be repaid, but it represents an equally valued income generating asset for those that hold it.**

- **Governments borrow by issuing and selling bonds, which pay the holder its stated value plus interest over an agreed period.**

- If the bond is issued in the sovereign currency of the nation, the default (non-payment) risk is negligible, as more money can always be created to finance payments.

- More borrowing can lead to inflation and the devaluation of a currency but not necessarily, as what matters is what it is spent on.

- Much like people and private organisations, countries have a credit rating based on their default risk and pay a higher interest rate if it is poor.

- Unlike private debt, public debt is not payable on demand by the holder and the bond can only be sold to someone else.

- The size of a nation's government debt doesn't really matter and neither does public debt (bonds) being owned by foreigners.

- Paying off national debt doesn't necessarily require the raising of taxes now or for future generations.

- The primary purpose of tax isn't to fund the government, it is to control inflation and to incentivise behaviour.

All debt is created money and government debt, also known as public or national debt, is no exception. Governments collect taxes from individuals and organisations, but for most of the time for most countries the expenditure of their government exceeds the tax revenues collected.[1] This means that governments need to borrow from individuals, organisations and even foreign governments to make up the shortfall. Bonds (or gilts as they are known) are issued to do this, which are basically IOUs that promise to pay the holder the specified value plus interest.

There are various types of government bonds that pay interest periodically, vary over time to maturity (when they are paid off), are inflation linked or are sold at a discount rather than pay interest.[2] Essentially all gilts can be converted to an equivalent and comparable 'yield' which is basically what interest it will return the holder over time. Much like a private loan, when the government issues bonds to fund expenditure it creates money. It is a newly created liability for the government and a newly created equivalent asset for the purchaser.

The UK national debt stood at approximately £2,365,400,000,000 (£2.4 trillion) in Q1 2022.[3] At 23.15 GMT on 28th August 2022, US National debt stood at about $30,742,744,500,000 ($30.7 trillion) and counting according to the website https://www.usdebtclock.org/, a rather anxiety producing live and ever rapidly increasing tally of US public debt. In comparison, gross domestic product (GDP) is the sum total of the value of all the goods and services produced by an entire country's economy in a year.

The below ONS graph[3] shows that for most rich countries the general gross government debt is close to or exceeds their entire nation's annual GDP, including the UK and US. The debt per taxpayer often significantly exceeds average incomes and, even without any 'new' borrowing for expenditure, the national debt will grow over time due to interest payments.

Figure 3: UK general government gross debt as a percentage of GDP at the end of December 2021 was lower than the G7 average

General government gross debt as a percentage of gross domestic product (GDP), at the end of December 2021, UK, EU and G7 member states

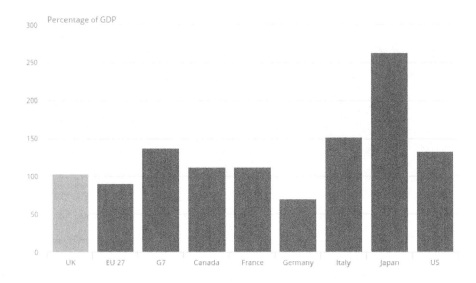

Source: Office for National Statistics[3]

You'd be forgiven for thinking that we're all screwed and that our grandchildren are going to have to hand over most of their income to pay our debts in the future. Indeed, that is often the sort of emotive language used by politicians to justify opposition to a particular government spending plan or to justify a general cutback in government expenditure (austerity). The quote at the start of this chapter from former UK Prime Minister Margaret Thatcher exemplifies the prevailing view of politicians across the political spectrum, that governments are like businesses and households that must eventually balance their books. However, it simply isn't true and is the main argument of Modern Monetary Theory, that ongoing deficits don't matter, can be sustained and are actually good for society.[4]

The government doesn't need the money of individuals or businesses now or in the future to pay off its debts or to continue to fund expenditure. As long as those debts are issued in the sovereign currency of the nation, it can always create more money to continue paying them. In this sense, the default (non-payment) risk of government bonds is negligible, which is why they often yield much less interest than corporate bonds (issued by companies), or the equivalent yields of stocks and shares of businesses, as they can and do go bust. Financial markets, whose main purpose is to correctly price risk into investments to maximise profits, nearly always view government debt as less risky than private sector debt for this reason.[5]

It is true that the issuance of new government bonds (creation of money for government expenditure including servicing existing debt) can create inflation and devalue the currency. There are famous historical examples of this such as in Germany between the World Wars and more recently in Zimbabwe and Venezuela, where hyperinflation was experienced and local money became virtually worthless due to a rapid creation of currency.[6]

It's also the case that a government will pay more interest on their debts if markets perceive them to be risky (there's a chance it won't meet bond obligations - usually down to a political choice or some sort of disaster / instability / sanctions / war).[5] They may also need to because so many bonds are issued that the return needs to be increased to find enough buyers. However, both outcomes do not necessarily occur as a result of increased government expenditure and borrowing, as is discussed below.

Inflation occurs in an economy when too much money is chasing too few goods, services and assets. Inflation can be demand driven or it can be supply driven and it is often caused by unexpected shocks, including policy choices.[7] For example, the government could half all employed peoples' income tax overnight if it chose to and suddenly give a significant boost to workers' take home pay. It could fund this newly created multi-billion shortfall in revenues with the issuance of bonds (creation of new money), which adds to the national debt. Although some people will choose to pay down personal debt (destroy the newly created money) with their extra pay, in net it's likely that households will increase their purchases of goods, services and assets (income generating investments such as stocks, shares and bonds).

However, the real productive resources of the economy are the same as before the tax cut and, although there would be some slack in production and inventories to meet increased demand, the result would likely be an increase in general prices and therefore inflation. Once these price rises take effect, people would be no better off as the new additional cash from the tax cut can only buy the same quantity and quality of goods, services and assets as before. No one is better off in real terms but the national debt is now billions higher. Therefore, tax cuts alone often do little to raise real prosperity and wellbeing.[8]

Despite this being a simplified example, if you dig a little deeper you will see that the inflation wasn't actually caused by the issuance of the bonds or an increase in the public debt. It was caused by what the newly created money was *used for* - to provide a new tax cut. Inflation was caused because the real productive resources and capacity of the economy weren't affected by the tax cut. The same labour, skills, technology, factories and assets were available after the new government borrowing and more money was chasing the same outputs.

A more pertinent example is a supply side shock causing inflation, as this is what we are currently living through in 2022. Following Putin's decision to invade Ukraine with Russian forces, the West has imposed various sanctions on the Russian Economy, which has restricted its ability to do business with the rest of the world. In response, Putin has been exploiting Europe's dependence on Russian oil and gas by cutting supplies to the continent. This has driven up their price and therefore overall inflation and the cost of living for Europe's citizens, with the intention of putting pressure on Western Governments to reduce sanctions and support of Ukraine. As the cost of oil and gas underpins the cost of many goods and services in an interlinked global system, it has caused inflation to spike in many countries including those outside of Europe, such as the US and the poorer nations of Africa and the Middle East.[9]

One of the key issues is that there aren't enough available alternatives to oil and natural gas in our economies as they underpin our heating, transport, agriculture, construction and energy sectors, and therefore indirectly impact all parts of the economy. It's possible to import more oil and gas from other parts of the world and this is what has happened since the war started. However, there are higher costs of transporting commodities over greater distances via ships (rather than via connected pipelines with Russia).

In addition, oil and gas producing countries such as those in the Middle East have chosen to not increase supply sufficiently to make up for the reduction in supply from Russia, thus maintaining the higher prices they are paid for each unit.[10] One option to mitigate the impacts of the supply shock on inflation is to increase domestic production in the West, such as from the US or UK and Norway in the North Sea, but doing so requires investment and time before it will have any sort of material impact. There are of course valid climate change and Net Zero target objections to doing so as well.

In response to this new cost of living crisis in 2022, governments have taken action to mitigate the impact on their electorates by doing things such as giving families money directly to offset against energy bills. While this eases the costs facing households in the short term (and is the right thing to do), it doesn't deal with the fundamental or long term issues of dependence on Russian oil and gas. Actions such as these are funded via windfall taxes on the large profits of energy companies as a result of the crisis or through additional borrowing.[11]

However, in addition to short term relief for households, western authorities could heavily invest in the infrastructure required for ultra low emission vehicles (electric, hydrogen, hybrid etc.) and offer generous incentives to encourage their take-up. They could also initiate a programme to insulate homes to high energy efficiency standards to reduce demand and the costs of heating. Governments could also invest in the production of renewable energy to reduce electricity costs, including more solar panels on homes to directly benefit households financially.

This could be accompanied by battery and electrolytic hydrogen production facilities to allow for hydrogen blending into gas grids, storage of energy seasonally and to smooth supply when renewables aren't producing. In addition, the resilience and base load of the grid could be significantly improved with an expansion of nuclear energy. A diversity of sources is needed for flexibility and reliability.

While taking some time to implement, this would all reduce reliance on imported oil and natural gas and should actually serve to reduce costs in the economy i.e. be non or even anti-inflationary. It would also contribute significantly to meeting Net Zero and Climate Change targets and likely generate significant economic growth and jobs. Recent research from Oxford University has suggested that the benefits of a swift transition to Net Zero is in the trillions, verses a slow or no transition.[12] Such a transition would largely delivered by the private sector, but could be significantly funded or at least incentivised by public money and policies. If the source of it was bonds (borrowing), this creation of new money wouldn't likely lead to significant and lasting inflation. It would actually expand and improve the productive resources of the economy i.e. it would have a real impact on wealth, resilience and wellbeing.

Therefore, government expenditure funded by the creation of money through bonds need not always be inflationary and targeted interventions can even be anti-inflationary. What matters is what the spending is used for and, as long as it increases the real productive capacity of the economy, it should raise overall real wellbeing and prosperity. Both fiscal and monetary policy can work together to control inflation and help our society thrive!

However, even if the creation of public debt does not always lead to inflation, should we as citizens be worried about the size and growth of public debt and whether or not it is owed to foreign individuals, organisations and even governments? Well, the short answer is no. When a government bond is created, it brings new sovereign money into existence and this is spent on the activities of government. As discussed, the gilt itself will promise to pay the holder a specified sum on a specified date (which can be in the next few years or decades in the future) plus interest. Alternatively, it is sold at less than the maturity value, which has the same effect as paying interest - giving the buyer a surplus or profit at the end of the period.[2]

Unlike a lot of private loans, the holder of the bond has no power to demand full payment of the maturity value plus interest early. They can only cash in those gilts for a penalty (forgone interest and at value today) or sell it to someone else.[13] Therefore, they have no real leverage over the government and cannot significantly affect what they must pay or when on that gilt. The liability for the government is exactly the same whether the original purchaser made a profit or not on the sale of the bond. The holders of national debt may be using the profits from it to undermine national and societal interests, which is a totally separate consideration and could just as easily apply to domestic holders of gilts as it does to foreign ones.

Therefore, non-domestic owners of bonds have no real power over the government from that ownership. Imagine a hypothetical scenario where a significant proportion of one country's bonds was owned by another, say US debt owned by China (they own less than 4% in reality!).[14] If those two nations' relations soured significantly and they stopped trading, the worst thing China could do would be to sell all their US bonds or cash them in at a penalty. This would reduce the price of US bonds and increase their yield. Therefore, any new debt needed for expenditure by the US would have to likely be paid at a (marginally) higher interest rate to find buyers, but that doesn't really matter as new dollars could be created to cover it.

In that situation, China would find themselves with a lot of dollars from the sale of those bonds which they would need to exchange for their own and / or other still friendly countries' currency to be of any use to them. The selling of dollars for Chinese and its allies' currencies would devalue the dollar and raise the value of their currencies, which would increase US export competitiveness and damage the export competitiveness, and thus economies, of China and its allies.[14]

Therefore, it doesn't really matter who owns government bonds denominated in its sovereign currency, as the worst thing a holder can do is sell them and potentially drive up interest costs of new bonds, and this is unlikely to be pain free for the seller. As mentioned previously, the only real consideration is whether the purchasers of gilts are using the profits from them to undermine national interest, in which case there may be a case to be more selective of who they are sold to.

The below ONS graph[15] shows the growth of public sector net debt since 1994 in the UK, as well as how the Bank of England has contributed to that debt more recently through Quantitative Easing (QE). QE is when the central bank creates money and directly purchases assets (mostly government bonds) in the economy from major financial institutions and pension funds.[16] The created demand for those assets increases their price and therefore lowers their yield (return or profit). The theory is this causes private institutions to instead purchase other assets such as the stocks and shares of companies to seek higher returns, which lowers the cost of borrowing for those companies and encourages them to spend and invest in the real economy.

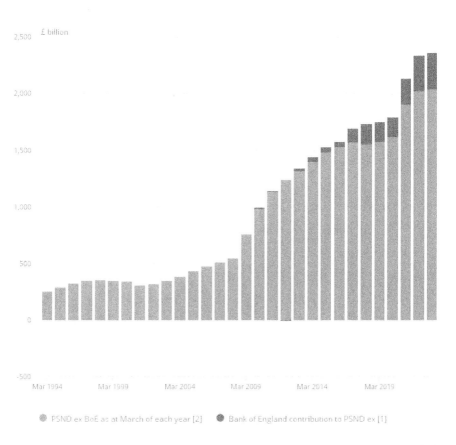

Figure 9: The Bank of England contributed £321.4 billion to public sector net debt at the end of May 2022

Public sector net debt excluding public sector banks, UK, March 1994 to the end of May 2022

- PSND ex BoE as at March of each year [2]   ● Bank of England contribution to PSND ex [1]

Source: Office for National Statistics[15]

Quantitative easing was commenced by central banks in the wake of the 2008 Financial Crisis to stimulate faltering economies and financial systems. Interest rates fell close to zero across the world following the crisis to try and restart economic growth in the aftermath. As rates couldn't go any lower (without turning negative, which is technically possible) and economic growth and inflation remained below target, QE was deemed necessary to provide further stimulus.[16]

In the above graph, the ONS records the £112.1 billion difference between the £843.8 billion of central bank reserves created to purchase the bonds and their £731.7 billion redemption value today as part of public sector net debt.[15] However, no private organisation outside of government is owed the value of the bonds held by the BoE (which is part of the public sector) and as the central bank it has no need for the money. If the government pays interest on the bonds or the value at maturity, the money is simply destroyed.

Therefore, the QE contribution to net debt is separated, as it is not true debt like that owed to private organisations, individuals and other governments. The opposite of QE is quantitative tightening, where the central bank sells their holdings of bonds back to the market, which reduces their price and increases their yield. This means there is less money available to the private sector as banks and funds hold relatively more of the low risk government gilts due to their higher returns. This should help reduce inflation as less is available for businesses to spend in the real economy.

Chart 2.4: Government spending during periods of conflict and peace

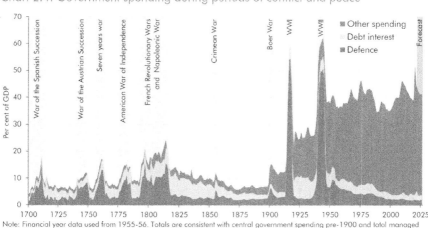

Note: Financial year data used from 1955-56. Totals are consistent with central government spending pre-1900 and total managed expenditure thereafter.
Source: Bank of England, HM Treasury, IFS, Mitchell, OBR

Source: Office of Budget Responsibility [17]

The above chart from the UK's Office of Budget Responsibility shows that, despite the recent significant rise in spending and debt, debt interest payments remain low as a proportion of GDP by historical standards.[17] This shows that the size of the national debt isn't necessarily correlated to how much interest is paid on it. Therefore, we shouldn't worry about the size of the national debt in and of itself. It is the market perception of a government that matters for the return they have to offer to sell bonds. Purchasers are more concerned with stability and general competence of the government and the growth of the economy and inflation, rather than the size of the debt itself.

The conclusion of everything in this chapter is that the creation of money via the issuance of government bonds for public expenditure is not necessarily inflationary, as it depends on what it is spent on. Foreign owners of national debt in the sovereign currency of a country have no power over the government and can only sell their bonds to someone else or cash them in for a penalty. The size of the public debt doesn't matter in and of itself and isn't always linked to how much interest the government pays on debt.

Paying off the national debt can always be done by creating more bonds (money) and therefore tax isn't necessary to pay the government debt now or in the future. People often say or hear about the 'taxpayers money' being spent (or more likely wasted) and that the 'taxpayer is on the hook' for expenditure now or in years to come. This still seems to be the prevailing view of politicians across the political spectrum and dominates the way national debt is spoken about in the media and literature.

However, what people and organisations are taxed is *always* a political choice and not a necessity. Taxation does not *have* *to* fund government expenditure. The government does not need our money as they can always create their own without limit.[4] Most politicians aren't being deceitful when they talk of their belief about the government not being able to afford something, but their point of view is usually due to a lack of understanding. The truth is the money can *always* be made available.

The creation of money via government bonds is only inflationary when it funds consumption or expenditure on fixed resources. It is wealth, prosperity, wellbeing and resilience enhancing when it increases the productive capacity of the economy and lowers the real costs (hours of labour, resource inputs etc.) to create economic outputs. The main purpose of taxation is actually to control inflation and to incentivise behaviour, i.e. make certain undesirable things from a public good perspective more expensive, such as 'sin' taxes on alcohol and cigarettes. This is the conclusion of Modern Monetary theory and what best describes reality.

To recap:

- **Public debt represents a liability for the government that must be repaid, but it represents an equally valued income generating asset for those that hold it.**

- **Governments borrow by issuing and selling bonds, which pay the holder its stated value plus interest over an agreed period.**

- **If the bond is issued in the sovereign currency of the nation, the default (non-payment) risk is negligible, as more money can always be created to finance payments.**

- More borrowing can lead to inflation and the devaluation of a currency but not necessarily, as what matters is what it is spent on.

- Much like people and private organisations, countries have a credit rating based on their default risk and pay a higher interest rate if it is poor.

- Unlike private debt, public debt is not payable on demand by the holder and the bond can only be sold to someone else.

- The size of a nation's government debt doesn't really matter and neither does public debt (bonds) being owned by foreigners.

- Paying off national debt doesn't necessarily require the raising of taxes now or for future generations.

- The primary purpose of tax isn't to fund the government, it is to control inflation and to incentivise behaviour.

Chapter 3 References

[1] Confronting Budget Deficits (International Monetary Fund)

[2] Treasury Securities & Programs (Treasury Direct)

[3] UK government debt and deficit: March 2022 (Office for National Statistics)

[4] The Deficit Myth: Modern Monetary Theory and How to Build a Better Economy, Kelton, 2020 (John Murray Publishers Ltd)

[5] Government Bonds (Brooks Macdonald)

[6] Worst Cases of Hyperinflation in History, Johnston, 2022 (Investopedia)

[7] What Causes Inflation and Who Profits From It?, 2022 (Investopedia)

[8] Keeping tax low for the rich does not boost economy, Hope & Limberg, 2020 (London School of Economics)

[9] Global inflation tracker: see how your country compares on rising prices, Romei & Smith, 2022 (Financial Times)

[10] Analysis: OPEC+ leaders like $100 oil, won't necessarily defend it, Lawler & Rashad, 2022 (Reuters)

[11] EU expects to raise €140bn from windfall tax on energy firms, Rankin & Lawson, 2022 (Guardian)

[12] Decarbonising the energy system by 2050 could save trillions - Oxford study, Way et al. 2022 (Oxford University)

[13] Time to Cash in Your U.S. Savings Bonds?, Daugherty, 2022 (Investopedia)

[14] Why China Buys U.S. Debt With Treasury Bonds, Seth, 2021 (Investopedia)

[15] Public sector finances, UK: July 2022 (Office for National Statistics)

[16] What is quantitative easing? (Bank of England)

[17] Fiscal risks and sustainability, July 2022 (Office for Budget Responsibility)

4. Should governments spend more than they do currently?

"There isn't a magic money tree that we can shake that suddenly provides for everything that people want"

Theresa May, UK Prime Minister

Key Points

- **The size of government debt doesn't matter and tax isn't needed to fund expenditure, but there are limits to what governments can spend responsibly.**

- **The constraints on spending are the real productive resources of the economy and inflation.**

- **Modern society is a complex system and governments aren't all knowing and all powerful.**

- Capitalism, private markets and decentralised decision making have generated more abundance than at any point in human history.

- However, we are threatening the natural systems on which we rely for survival and far too many people are facing poverty.

- People are at the centre of the economy and the goal of economic activity should be to maximise their wellbeing and prosperity in a sustainable way.

- The key issue is putting our productive resources to their best use and expanding those resources so we can do more with our created money in a non-inflationary way.

- There is an overwhelming case that economies across the world are nowhere near optimal resource allocation and that government expenditure could and should significantly increase.

- There needs to be checks and balances on government expenditure - democratic, fiscal and monetary oversight.

The previous chapter argued that bond funded government expenditure won't necessarily cause inflation, if carefully targeted on reducing costs and raising economic output. In addition, the size of the national debt doesn't matter and tax isn't necessary to fund government expenditure now or in the future. If we accept this as true, then what does this say about the case for more government investment and spending on the things we need to thrive as a society? Are there any limits on what the government could and should spend to give us everything that we want and need? Or is there really a magic money tree!?

As discussed previously, the constraints are the real productive resources of the economy and inflation. The real economy includes the labour available and their skills and knowledge, the manufacturing capacity of factories and businesses, the technology available to turn inputs into outputs, energy production, the quantity and quality of farmland and any natural resources such as oil, gas, fish and the ecosystems that provide various services for free, such as pollination of crops and climate control.[1]

People are at the centre of the economy and maximisation of their wellbeing and prosperity in a sustainable way should be the ultimate purpose of all economic activity. Human productivity is underpinned by our health, nutrition, happiness, social networks, education, recreation opportunities, a healthy environment and protection from threats such as violence, crime, floods and weather etc. The provision of all of this requires significant expenditure and often on activities that it is not easy or even possible to make a profit from; and therefore can't be provided effectively by the private sector alone.[2]

However, modern society is a large and complex system with many needs and wants. The government isn't an all knowing and all powerful entity that knows exactly what its people desire. The more decentralised and market based economies of the West emerged from the Cold War much better off than the centrally planned economies of the Soviet Union and its allies. This was because people were free to make decisions locally and for themselves. Capitalism and private markets based on competition and self-interest have produced wondrous things and, on many measures (lifespan, technology, availability of food and shelter, medical care, recreational opportunities etc.), there has never been a better time to be alive.[3]

However, despite there being more abundance than at any point in human history, far too many people still live in poverty and don't have access to basic provisions or have the opportunity to improve their lives. This is the case both internationally and within countries, including the richest. We are undermining the sustainability and even existence of our society by degrading the natural environment on which it depends through pollution (including greenhouse gas emissions) and habitat destruction with associated biodiversity loss. The significant inequalities within and between countries also undermine peace and stability. People and nations who feel like they have nothing to lose are more likely to resort to violence, crime and the destruction of property and natural environments, as they are focused on short term survival and motivated by resentment.

Therefore, there is a need for all of us to create and make available the necessary money to ensure that society can thrive over time. We have had the power since 1971 and the end of the gold standard to create unlimited quantities of currency to fund spending on things that improve our lives. Financial and wider technology has now reached a point where we can fully unleash the potential of this reality in a non-inflationary and real prosperity enhancing way. Most people, including politicians, still view the government as a business or household that must eventually balance its books but, as explained in previous chapters, this simply isn't the case as the issuer of sovereign currency.

The questions we should be asking are:

- Is our economy at full capacity and are our resources allocated to their most valuable use?

- Are we investing enough in the protection and restoration of our natural environment?

- What investments can we make to improve productivity, so as to produce more and better goods, services and assets from our available inputs?

- How can we continually expand our productive capacity so we can do more with our created money?

If we take off the self imposed shackles of our government's finances, we can begin to maximise the potential of our societies. Economies across the world are nowhere near their productive capacities. The below graph from the ONS shows that UK unemployment as of June 2022 is 3.8%, the lowest it has been since late 1974 and something which has been hailed as a 'jobs miracle'.[4] This suggests that the labour component of our economic capacity is at or close to its maximum.

However, the unemployment rate only estimates those officially and actively seeking work. The converse employment rate includes those on temporary and zero hour contracts, underemployed (in a role below their skill and potential wage level), part-time workers and self-employed (entrepreneurs, gig economy workers and contractors). It says nothing about the general quality and security of their employment and whether people are optimally matched to their preferences, skills and the needs of society.

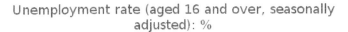

Unemployment rate (aged 16 and over, seasonally adjusted): %

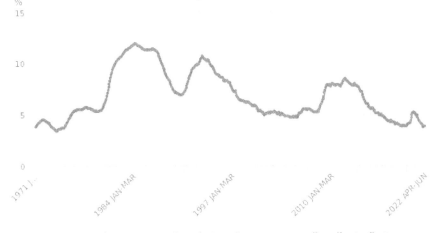

—— Unemployment rate (aged 16 and over, seasonally adjusted): %

Source: Office for National Statistics[4]

In addition, the following ONS graph on economic inactivity shows that 8.9 million people are currently not employed and not officially seeking work. This is 21%, or over 1 in 5, of the UK's 16-64 population. While around 30% of those in are students in education, the rest are out of the workforce for reasons ranging from disability and sickness to homemakers, early retirees and those simply discouraged from work.[5] For some people this is likely to be a choice, but for others it will be born out of necessity or circumstances outside of their control.

There are likely to be a significant proportion of the officially employed, unemployed and economically inactive that would like more and better work closer aligned to their preferences and skills, at the hours they would like and that is more secure than what is available currently. There are plenty of others that would like to start their own businesses but can't because they don't have access to the financial resources, affordable care and support necessary (which may be for themselves, loved ones or their children).

There will also be plenty of over 64s, who aren't even included in those statistics, willing and able to work, wanting to start their own businesses or even just happy to volunteer their time, but can't for the same reasons. Therefore, despite the official unemployment rate painting a relatively rosy picture for the UK (which may not last itself with the upcoming recession!), there is evidence of a significant proportion of labour not or under utilised. This is the case in every country globally, many of which already have poor headline unemployment to start with. Unlike other components of our economic capacity, let us not forget that labour is people with desires, preferences, needs and autonomy, so it is about giving them opportunities and choices to fulfill their potential, rather than making them work against their will or for wages insufficient to live a dignified life.

LFS: Economically Inactive: UK: All: Aged 16-64: Thousands: SA

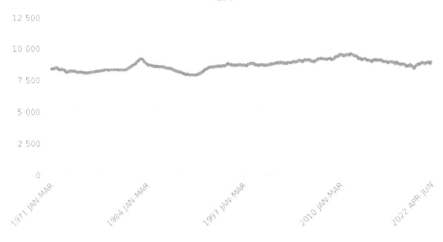

—•— LFS: Economically Inactive: UK: All: Aged 16-64: Thousands: SA

Source: Office for National Statistics[5]

The current supply driven inflation shock, which is driving the global economy towards recession, is actually an opportunity for a step change in government investment in an anti-inflationary way. If we reduce the costs of buying, renting and running homes, feeding families, of transport, of healthcare, of social care, of child care, we can free people's talents and their resources to fulfill their potential.

We can also properly fund the protection and the restoration of our natural environment and ecosystems, so that we can continue to benefit from their many services to humanity long into the future.[2] We can take the necessary action to reduce pollution and emissions, adapt to the climate change already locked in and become more resilient and prosperous in the process.[6]

The government can't do all of this on its own and all parts of society, individuals and private organisations will have to do their part. The next chapter discusses the role of people and the private sector in ensuring the prosperity of society. However, there is an overwhelming case for government expenditure to significantly increase to tackle all the issues facing the global community and to properly fund things like our education, healthcare and a myriad of other things. This is pro environment, pro wealth, pro business, pro wellbeing, pro growth and pro freedom. Given the reality of public debt and money creation as revealed by MMT, it is a no brainer.

Despite this demonstrable need, there should be checks and balances on public expenditure to ensure it is responsible and focuses on the most pressing priorities first. One check and balance is the democratic process. In the parts of the world fortunate enough to have free and fair elections, governments propose their spending programme and the people vote for the party which most appeals to their preferences and values. The risk of losing office should help ensure that governments keep the people's interests at the heart of their decision making.

However, democratic oversight could always be strengthened with things like citizen panels feeding into spending plans and better funding and utilisation of local government or other decentralised organisations to decide where investment can best meet local priorities. Of course, widespread education on the reality of money creation and government expenditure itself will go a long way to influence voters and politicians to do more with the resources of the nation.

On the fiscal programme, governments can and have set up independent oversight bodies to scrutinise government expenditure, to ensure it is being spent wisely and to tell governments how much 'fiscal headroom' they have in budgets. In the UK, there is the Office of Budget Responsibility (OBR), which independently forecasts the economic outlook, tax receipts and any fiscal risks.[7]

The government sets spending rules such as ensuring that public debt doesn't grow as a proportion of GDP, which allows the OBR to estimate what budget is available given allowed borrowing within the rules, forecast GDP and forecast tax receipts. The rules could be relaxed to allow greater government spending with a MMT perspective, but the remit of the OBR could be retained and modified to account for forecast inflation becoming a limiting factor on expenditure. Planned investments that would reduce inflation by expanding the productive capacity of the economy could create forecast 'monetary headroom' in addition to fiscal headroom in government budgets.

A final check and balance is one that is already in place. That is the inflation target and independence of central banks. If government expenditure is inflationary then the central bank will continue to have the power to raise interest rates or use QE / QT to bring inflation back towards target. This should disincentivise governments from overspending or spending on consumption (e.g. via tax cuts) without increasing the productive capacity of the economy.

Increasing interest rates would hurt the electorate and therefore damage the prospects of the government being reelected. However, there may be a case to raise the inflation target (e.g. up to 5%) to allow for greater government expenditure without increasing interest rates. As long as real wealth, productivity and incomes increase by more than this, people will be better off in real terms over time. If real purchasing power is increasing or at least being maintained, whether inflation is 2% or 5% doesn't matter. However, this absolutely must be the case for the poorest in society as they are the ones who suffer most from price rises.

The central bank could also be given a supplementary remit to keep government interest payments as low as possible by directly buying new bonds (instead of existing bonds off the market as with QE) when there is sufficient monetary and inflationary headroom. This would reduce the supply of government bonds going to the market and thus increase their price and therefore reduce their yield (interest). Private institutions would have to seek returns elsewhere and invest in businesses bonds and shares, which would stimulate private investment. Whether this was feasible or desirable in practice will have to be explored further and the mechanism would have to be carefully calibrated, but it is certainly an idea worth considering.

Overall, the combination of the above should ensure the government's expenditure is responsible in a world where we accept that the level of debt doesn't matter and that government expenditure should significantly increase to raise the wellbeing and productivity of society. The detail of what this significantly increased government budget should be spent on is a political discussion that reflects the needs, values, culture and desires of each country. This will be refined by democratic process. The key challenge is convincing people and politicians that Modern Monetary Theory best describes the way our financial system works so we can remove the self imposed shackles of government expenditure, solve our significant societal challenges and realise our potential to thrive!

To recap:

- **The size of government debt doesn't matter and tax isn't needed to fund expenditure, but there are limits to what governments can spend responsibly.**

- **The constraints on spending are the real productive resources of the economy and inflation.**

- **Modern society is a complex system and governments aren't all knowing and all powerful.**

- Capitalism, private markets and decentralised decision making have generated more abundance than at any point in human history.

- However, we are threatening the natural systems on which we rely for survival and far too many people are facing poverty.

- People are at the centre of the economy and the goal of economic activity should be to maximise their wellbeing and prosperity in a sustainable way.

- The key issue is putting our productive resources to their best use and expanding those resources so we can do more with our created money in a non-inflationary way.

- There is an overwhelming case that economies across the world are nowhere near optimal resource allocation and that government expenditure could and should significantly increase.

- There needs to be checks and balances on government expenditure - democratic, fiscal and monetary oversight.

Chapter 4 References

[1] The Deficit Myth: Modern Monetary Theory and How to Build a Better Economy, Kelton, 2020 (John Murray Publishers Ltd)

[2] Paying Ourselves to Save the Planet - A Layman's Explanation of Modern Money Theory - J.D. Alt, 2020

[3] Enlightenment Now: The Case for Reason, Science, Humanism, and Progress, Pinker, 2019 (Penguin)

[4] Unemployment (Office for National Statistics)

[5] Economic inactivity (Office for National Statistics)

[6] Decarbonising the energy system by 2050 could save trillions - Oxford study, Way et al. 2022 (Oxford University)

[7] What we do (Office for Budget Responsibility)

5. The role of individuals and private organizations

"You cannot hope to build a better world without improving the individuals. To that end, each of us must work for his own improvement and, at the same time, share a general responsibility for all humanity, our particular duty being to aid those to whom we think we can be most useful."

Marie Curie, physicist who laid the foundations for cancer treatment

Key Points

- **Private organisations and individuals have the power to create money and do so whenever they take out loans or buy things on credit.**

- **With this power comes just as much responsibility as governments for our collective wellbeing.**

- The choices you make matter and have far reaching impacts in our interconnected society, so it is important to spend ethically and responsibly.

- The limits to how much individuals and organisations can safely borrow are determined by the interest rate and what the money is used for.

- As with governments, individuals and the private sector should avoid borrowing for consumption where possible and instead use debt to invest in reducing costs, expanding productive capacity and to create or obtain income generating assets.

- If you are fortunate enough to have a growing or stable monthly financial surplus, consider donating a proportion to charity to help others.

- As the national debt doesn't matter, individuals and private organisations should use all legal means, deductions and credits to avoid paying tax and claim all benefits entitled to (as the rich actively do already!).

- **The government should create conditions and incentives for individuals and organisations to be financially responsible and secure.**

- **Individuals and businesses have a duty to proactively fight inflation by shopping around for the best deals, minimising their costs, charging fair prices and investing wisely.**

As discussed in the chapter on money creation, individuals and private organisations create money when we take out loans or buy goods, services and assets on credit. There is a new liability for the borrower and a new asset for the lender that wasn't there previously. This new currency is brought into existence and with this power comes as much responsibility as governments for our collective wellbeing. The impact of credit based consumption expenditure is the same whether it is done by the private or public sector, and is just as likely to be inflationary. Equally, the paying down of debts is the destruction of money and overall likely to be anti-inflationary.

As all money is debt, income from the sale of goods and services, employment, assets and / or the government ultimately comes from borrowing. Therefore, even expenditure from 'debt free' households is based on loan created currency and comes with the same social impacts and obligations. Overall, the private sector has a bigger influence on inflation and societal wellbeing than the public sector due to its relative size and through our choices and creation of money. This is because, as well as the direct consequences of our expenditure, the public and businesses have a significant impact on government spending choices through the democratic process and via the tax revenues our activities generate.[1]

Therefore, the financial choices you make matter and have far reaching impacts in our interconnected society, so it is important to spend ethically and responsibly. Where the goods and services you buy are sourced from are important, as certain products have significant environmental and social impacts (both positive and negative). We all have personal carbon, resource, social and financial (inflation) footprints that give or take away from the wellbeing of society, and so do the organisations we own and work for.[2]

You are personally responsible for living within your means, even if you can't always control events that may affect your ability to do so. For example, unexpected health issues may prevent you from earning an income or an external supply shock due to a natural disaster or geopolitical events may cause the costs of living to be suddenly very expensive, as we are experiencing in 2022. An external event could even result in the destruction of your home and livelihood such as floods and fire, as is the case for far too many people across the world.

As much as is in your control, you are responsible for looking after your physical and mental health and that of those around you as much as you can. You have an obligation to minimise your costs to society by not committing crimes, ripping people off, eating as healthily as you can, exercising as much as your body allows, avoiding substance and alcohol abuse and not consuming more than you need. The same can be said of the private organisations we work for and own, which should aim to have a net positive impact on society and the environment.[3]

However, it's not all about our obligations and responsibilities. You have a right to a happy and fulfilling life filled with rich experiences and you also have a right to build your wealth if you can. Debt (created money) can be a tool to do so, but it needs to be used responsibly. You can't avoid taking measured risks in life and sometimes you need to borrow in order to start businesses, purchase your home or a car, to buy income generating (or cost reducing) assets and even to cover shortfalls in emergencies. If we expect our government to borrow to invest in society to improve the productive capacity of our economy, its sustainability and to raise the wellbeing of everyone, then we as private individuals and organisations should do so as well.[4]

However, unlike the government, the limits to how much individuals and organisations can safely borrow are harder, as we must find income from elsewhere to pay debts off and there are significant consequences of not being able to repay, such as bankruptcy or even jail. Lower interest rates lower the risk of borrowing as it means less income needs to be found to meet repayments. However, borrowing is inherently more risky for individuals and private organisations and should only be done when absolutely necessary, and ideally as a carefully considered investment to improve your financial situation in the long term.[4]

Seeking professional advice and doing thorough research will help individuals determine what is best to spend their money on to raise their own and other's prosperity. However, things like starting businesses that provide real value to people, purchasing cost saving investments such as solar panels and energy efficiency measures, creating and producing valued content for others and investing in your own skills and knowledge will likely help you navigate life's challenges better. Such choices will hopefully ensure you are a net contributor to social wellbeing.

If you are fortunate enough to have a financial surplus available each month, it is worth considering donating a proportion of it (say 10%) to charity to help those less well off than you or to a particular cause close to your heart, such as environmental ones. If you are able to grow your financial surplus over time you can then also grow your charitable contributions. It is very rewarding to see the money you have created and made available help others, and it also improves your life by contributing to the community and environment you live in.[5]

As discussed in previous chapters, the size of the national debt doesn't matter and taxation isn't needed for government expenditure. Therefore, there is nothing wrong with individuals and businesses exploiting all legal means at their disposal to minimise the tax they pay. For example, taking advantage of tax deductions (such as for charitable giving or expenses), tax credits, any benefits you are entitled to and arranging your financial affairs in a tax minimising way, which is likely to require professional advice.

There is often a significant stigma in doing so in poorer communities with associated shaming, but the open secret is this is exactly what the rich do! They and large businesses often pay lower effective tax rates than less well off segments of society and smaller businesses, as they spend a lot on experts who can legally (and sometimes not so!) find ways for them to avoid paying tax.[6] This might not be fair or optimal for the overall wellbeing of society and there is a case for the government to close tax loopholes for the rich and large organisations. How we can potentially review our tax system is considered in the next chapter, but suffice to say there is nothing wrong with legally minimising your tax burden so you have more to spend on the things that matter to you and that contribute to your community.

The government has a clear role in creating the right conditions and incentives for individuals and private organisations to be financially self-sufficient and responsible. They should also act as the safety net for households when things go wrong. The benefits available should be sufficient for everyone to live a dignified life if they are unable to provide for themselves financially or are undergoing hardship due to events outside of their control. The overall goal is for individuals, the private sector and public sector to work together to create a kinder, safer, resilient, sustainable and prosperous society.

As has been covered, inflation erodes the real purchasing power of individuals and organisations and it also limits what the government can spend to provide us with public services and infrastructure. Therefore, we all must pay our part in proactively keeping it down by shopping around for the best deals, minimising our costs, charging fair prices and investing wisely. If we avoid waste and excess consumption, paying unfair prices, and choosing to shop ethically and sustainably, businesses will respond to our choices and provide more of what we want and ask for through our purchases.

We can't expect the government to shoulder all of the burden, even if there is eventually widespread acceptance of the conclusions of Modern Monetary Theory and the realities of our financial system. The private sector has the same power as governments to create money (but the constraints of debt are harder), so MMT implies a significant role for us all.

To recap:

- **Private organisations and individuals have the power to create money and do so whenever they take out loans or buy things on credit.**

- **With this power comes just as much responsibility as governments for our collective wellbeing.**

- **The choices you make matter and have far reaching impacts in our interconnected society, so it is important to spend ethically and responsibly.**

- **The limits to how much individuals and organisations can safely borrow are determined by the interest rate and what the money is used for.**

- As with governments, individuals and the private sector should avoid borrowing for consumption where possible and instead use debt to invest in reducing costs, expanding productive capacity and to create or obtain income generating assets.

- If you are fortunate enough to have a growing or stable monthly financial surplus, consider donating a proportion to charity to help others.

- As the national debt doesn't matter, individuals and private organisations should use all legal means, deductions and credits to avoid paying tax and claim all benefits entitled to (as the rich actively do already!).

- The government should create conditions and incentives for individuals and organisations to be financially responsible and secure.

- Individuals and businesses have a duty to proactively fight inflation by shopping around for the best deals, minimising their costs, charging fair prices and investing wisely.

Chapter 5 References

[1] IMF Survey : IMF Facilitates Debate on Private Sector, Growth, Jobs in Mideast, 2013 (International Monetary Fund)

[2] Ethical finance - a focus for 2021 and beyond, McMillan & McVey, 2021 (Scottish Business Insider)

[3] PSR v CSR: Is personal social responsibility still good for business?, Devalia, 2009 (My Customer)

[4] How to use debt to build wealth, 2022, (US Bank)

[5] How much should I give to charity?, 2019 (GoodBox)

[6] The Forbes 400 Pay Lower Tax Rates Than Many Ordinary Americans, Hanlon & Buffie, 2021 (American Progress)

6. Other considerations

"The ideas of economists and political philosophers, both when they are right and when they are wrong, are more powerful than is generally understood. Indeed, the world is ruled by little else."

John Maynard Keynes, Economist

This penultimate chapter includes summaries of a few economic concepts and ideas that could be tried or at least considered as a result of hopefully widespread acceptance of Modern Monetary Theory. If we acknowledge as a society the realities of money creation and national debt, we can give ourselves the space to significantly increase public and private expenditure to try and realise our potential as a species and secure a prosperous future for us all. Doing so will allow us to be more creative, innovative and experimental with what we spend money on and how we fund things. Each concept covered in this chapter is worthy of a book in and of itself and, where accessible works are available, I have included recommended reading.

Tax and Benefits Reform

Taxes and subsidies make certain things more expensive and cheaper respectively, and therefore have a significant impact on incentives and behaviour. They also help control inflation by reducing the money available for goods and services. While the previous chapters have demonstrated that taxation is not necessary to fund government expenditure, it remains an important and essential tool of government to enhance social wellbeing and to influence the behaviour of organisations and individuals.

Tax in the UK (and other major economies) mainly comes from Income, National Insurance Contributions (or healthcare equivalent), VAT and businesses' profits.[1] This effectively reduces people's and companies' incentives to earn income as it means the return from labour and entrepreneurial activity is lower than it would otherwise be. It can also discourage people from coming off benefits by finding work, as they are sometimes only marginally better off from doing so due to the tax they pay on the money they earn. In addition, National Insurance Contributions make it more expensive for businesses to hire labour and discourage them from creating as many jobs as they otherwise would.

There are various and innovative ways to reform our tax system to make it fairer, more sustainable and wellbeing enhancing. For example, the tax base could be shifted from incomes to consumption and pollution. This could be a way to address inequalities and give more money to the poorest (and the middle class) in society, by only having the very richest segments of the population pay any income tax. This would mean more money is available for the majority of society. This could be used to offset a transitory increase in the cost of goods and services caused by imposing pollution taxes to reflect carbon emissions and other environmental costs. [2]

This would have to be supplemented by a more generous benefits system to ensure those not able or temporarily not working are still able to afford a reasonable and dignified standard of living. The result of shifting taxes from incomes to consumption and pollution would be to encourage less resource intensive and environmentally damaging purchases and activities. Over time, this would harness the power of markets to reduce our environmental impact as those businesses able to provide goods and services at least cost to the natural world (and therefore people) would have a competitive advantage and increased market share. [2]

In addition, more land or wealth taxes could be applied to encourage optimal use of land and capital, which may be to divert them to nature or to allow the building of affordable homes where there is a shortage. Allowing more breathing space in government budgets through adoption of a MMT perspective would create the opportunity for such significant changes to taxation to be tried and gradually implemented so as to manage transitory risks.

Recommended books:

- *What Everyone Needs to Know about Tax - An Introduction to the UK Tax System* by James Hannam

- *The Joy of Tax* by Richard Murphy

Universal Basic Income

A step further than fundamental taxation and benefits reform could be to abolish most means tested benefits and to give all citizens a right to a Universal Basic Income (UBI). This is where each person is paid a regular allowance sufficient to meet a basic baseline standard of living. It should ensure that no one is ever in poverty and can at least meet their essential needs whether they earn any additional income or not. While you may think this would encourage people to be lazy and disincentivise entrepreneurial activity and employment seeking, study after study have shown that it enhances economic activity and wellbeing in the areas it is tried.[3]

With the growth and development of AI and automation, UBI is being increasingly advocated as a necessary and desirable policy to counter the reduced need for people to produce goods and services. It could free people up to be creative, follow recreational pursuits, volunteer for social and environmental causes and to start their own businesses. It also guarantees a baseline level of demand for the private sector which should act to stabilise revenues in a future where robots and AI may be replacing significant quantities of human jobs.

There are incremental steps to full UBI which could be trialed to prove that it works on a large scale and can be sustainably funded with MMT principles and taxation reform. For example, a basic income for the poorest in society or trials in certain locations could develop evidence and support for the policy more widely, before full UBI is eventually implemented.

Recommended books:

- *Basic Income: And How We Can Make It Happen* by Guy Standing

- *Let There Be Money: Understanding Modern Monetary Theory and Basic Income* by Scott Stantens

Natural Capital Accounting

Human life and civilisation cannot survive without a healthy natural environment and stable climate. Pollution and resource exploitation from our economic activity is responsible for widespread habitat destruction, biodiversity loss and climate change. We are undermining the systems on which we rely for food, climate control, clean air, recreation, medicines and wellbeing. Our technology often takes inspiration from nature as well and is much more advanced as a result, such as mimicking bird wings to improve the efficiency of planes and shark skin to reduce the drag of materials in water.[4]

The reason for all of this degradation is that businesses and individuals who act in a sustainable and environmentally responsible way often face higher costs and cannot compete with those that overexploit the natural world. Therefore, there are incentives to pollute and destroy habitats and ecosystems for short term survival and gain.[5] Habitats can be thought of as a stock of natural capital that must be maintained, enhanced and expanded like other forms of capital that businesses interact with and manage. From these stocks are flows of ecosystem services that benefit humanity and are often provided for free or at a cost much lower than their true value.[6]

In combination with standard accounting techniques, which give a framework to properly manage our natural capital and ecosystem services in a way that is understood by businesses and governments, we can use valuation methods to properly assess the worth of these assets. Their true value simply isn't reflected by market prices and so must be inferred by the avoided cost of humans producing the equivalent outputs (if we even can!), the actions of people in relation to their use (revealed preference) or by surveys which derive our willingness to pay for them (stated preference). However, scientists advising politicians, and not economists, should set the hard planetary and ecological limits of our economic activity.[7]

The protection and restoration of our natural capital (habitats) and their ecosystem services is going to require significant funding, largely from the public sector. This is because it is difficult to make a profit from doing so as you can't easily exclude and therefore charge people for access to, or use of, public goods like our natural environment (and neither should we!). Therefore, a Natural Capital Accounting Framework can help society assess how the stock of environmental goods and services changes over time. This can identify targets and where investment is needed the most to restore systems to a state that is sustainable and maximises benefits for us all.

Recommended books:

- *Natural Capital: Valuing the Planet* by Dieter Helm

- *What Has Nature Ever Done for Us?: How Money Really Does Grow On Trees* by Tony Jupiter

Defence, Foreign Aid and Democracy

This book is largely written from the perspective of the relatively wealthy UK, a country fortunate enough to have free and fair elections (despite there always being room to improve and strengthen our democratic processes!). We and the countries like us enjoy freedoms that are the envy of many in the world. However, they are also under constant threat from authoritarian forces at home and abroad and the price of democracy is constant vigilance against its erosion. Unfortunately we have not reached a point in our collective evolution where war between nations is a thing of the past, as demonstrated by Russia's invasion of Ukraine. There are potential conflict flashpoints around the world and the liberal democracies must work together to enhance their deterrents against aggression and to protect and encourage the spread of the freedoms we enjoy and take for granted.

All of this requires significant expenditure on both defence and foreign aid. An MMT perspective on national finances makes the allocation of funds to this an easier prospect for electorates to stomach and also means that it doesn't have to be at the expense of domestic priorities and needs. If we significantly expand the financial resources available for spending at home through the creation of money, we can also do so for our protection and to help those around the world that need it the most.

It opens up the possibility of debt forgiveness of poorer nations, especially those with legacy debts denominated in rich countries' currencies. These cripple developing countries' ability to lift themselves out of poverty and cause instability and resentment. We can also pay poorer nations to preserve the significant and globally important natural habitats that are located in their countries and help them develop in an environmentally sustainable way. We can tie this to conditions of democratic and socially responsible reforms to improve the rights and wellbeing of people in those nations. This can hopefully reduce poverty worldwide, raise prosperity and wellbeing and reverse the growing flow of refugees globally, to the benefit of us all.[8][9]

Chapter 6 References

[1] Where does the government get its money? (Institute for Fiscal Studies Tax Lab)

[2] Five facts about environmental taxes, 2018, (Office for National Statistics)

[3] Everywhere basic income has been tried, in one map, Samuel, 2020 (Vox)

[4] What is biomimicry?, 2022 (Biomimicry Institute)

[5] Tragedy of the Commons: What It Means in Economics, 2022 (Investopedia)

[6] What is natural capital?, 2022 (Natural Capital Forum)

[7] Principles of Natural Capital Accounting, 2017 (Office for National Statistics)

[8] Debt Relief Under the Heavily Indebted Poor Countries (HIPC) Initiative, 2016 (International Monetary Fund)

[9] A "debt standstill" for the poorest countries: How much is at stake?, 2020 (The Organisation for Economic Co-operation and Development)

Conclusions and what next?

"The future depends on what you do in the present"

Mahatma Gandhi, Indian lawyer, anti-colonial nationalist and nonviolent resistance advocate

"Modern Monetary Theory is not something you do, it is something that is!"

Bill Mitchell, Economist

It may seem counterintuitive to write a book advocating that we shouldn't worry about the size of national debt, and that a key limitation of government spending is inflation, in the middle of a significant inflation spike. However, this is the perfect time for significant government and private investment to address the supply side issues that are causing the current cost of living crisis.

We also need to provide immediate and comprehensive financial support to families and households to get them through the emergency situation we are facing in the upcoming winter and beyond. If we do not, there are likely to be excess and preventable winter deaths, as well as bankruptcies, home repossessions and permanent economic scarring from the severe recession that is likely to materialise.

In the world today, money has no intrinsic value and is created from nothing by the issuance of loans in the private sector or through bonds in the public sector. The overwhelming majority of money in existence is simply digits in computers. Therefore, money is literally no object. It is a created tool that facilitates trade and cooperation and is secondary in importance to the wellbeing, safety and prosperity of people, as well as the health and sustainability of our natural environment. There is a mantra of the rich that 'cash is trash' and they especially understand that money itself is not the source of wealth. It only imperfectly measures wealth at best.

Our ability to produce goods and services and create income generating assets is the source of our prosperity, as are the social networks and the environment on which we rely. Millionaires and billionaires do not have their fortunes as cash in the bank as they know it is constantly being eroded by inflation and the returns offered are meager. They instead create or purchase assets such as businesses, bonds and real estate which generate a flow of income or increase in value above inflation. This knowledge gap and ability to compound existing wealth is a significant factor in growing inequalities that are undermining social cohesion globally.

It's time that the truth about money was more widely known and that there was a general acceptance that the public and private sectors should work together to raise the productive capacity of the economy for everyone's benefit. To do this the government should properly fund public services such as education, healthcare, social care and childcare to free people to maximise their potential. They should also create the right incentives and conditions for individuals to be financially secure and responsible.

We need all of our ideas and talents unleashed to tackle the significant challenges of climate change and environmental degradation, as well as those of poverty, international relations, defending freedom and respecting human rights worldwide. The aim of this book is to change the political discourse from one about affordability to one about what we can do with our available resources and how we can expand those resources so we can do more over time with the money we create from nothing.

It has hopefully shown that we can afford to tackle these issues without resulting in rampant inflation or raising taxes significantly either now or for future generations. These are the conclusions of MMT and people like Professor Stephanie Kelton in *The Deficit Myth: Modern Monetary Theory and How to Build a Better Economy*. Governments do not need taxation to fund expenditure now or in the future, deficits can be maintained indefinitely and are actually good for society.

Tax does remain an important tool to control inflation and to incentivise behaviour. It also has a valuable redistributive purpose and MMT doesn't give the rich a get out of jail free card. Some inequality is unavoidable, and is even desirable, but it can also reach a level where it is harmful to democracy, wealth creation and social cohesion. We are at that point, and need tax reform to redistribute wealth more fairly and support those in need. This is inevitably a political conversation and different countries will arrive at different conclusions and compromise as to what is their preferred balance of taxation across society.

There was once a time when there was significant political focus and worry about the balance of payments of countries, but it hardly gets a mention anymore. This is where nations import more than they export and must fund the difference with inflows of capital.[8] These inflows purchase domestic assets and effectively loan importers money to continue trade deficits and generally maintain exchange rates.

Countries like the US and UK have continually ran current account deficits with the rest of the world and have relied on foreign direct investment, including the purchasing of government bonds, to be able to continually pay for the imported goods and services. There was once a question about whether this was desirable and sustainable to maintain in the long run.

However, now it is generally accepted that this can be continued indefinitely, as long as exchange rates are freely floating and international markets retain confidence in countries, as they are controlling inflation and growing in GDP (thus continually creating assets to invest in). The same is exactly true of government deficits. I believe that one day the discourse and focus will shift away from worry about public debt, and an assumption that taxation must eventually rise to balance government books, to one about how to invest in the right things to grow our productive capacity and control inflation.

The first country or countries to fully embrace a MMT outlook when running their economy are likely to test the confidence of international financial markets. They may experience some turbulence and devaluation of their currencies if significantly increased public expenditure is not done carefully. It is therefore essential that the democratic, fiscal and monetary checks and balances discussed are maintained and strengthened, especially retaining an independent central bank charged with controlling inflation.

Controlling general price rises by increasing interest rates is one of the most painful and destructive ways to do so. It would be much better to bring down inflation with technology and productivity improvements driven by targeted investments. The need to raise interest rates due to inflation is a sign that society isn't spending money wisely (both the public and private sectors).

MMT is not necessarily a perspective of the left or right of the political spectrum and is about expanding the financial resources available to spend on what matters to each country. It is about recognising the realities of the financial system and doing what you think is best with that knowledge. The expansion of available government budgets (whether used or not by the party in power) needs to be carefully managed with the messaging around it carefully framed, just as is the case when central banks set interest rate expectations so as not to spook financial markets. Fiscal policy and monetary policy can and must work hand in hand to raise our prosperity and control inflation. This includes the proper protection and restoration of our natural environment.

As discussed, individuals and the private sector have the most significant role to play in ensuring our collective wellbeing and prosperity into the future. We have the same power as governments to create money from debt and therefore the same responsibilities with that power. We should only consume what we need to, take on debt if absolutely necessary and ideally only use it to fund the improvement of our financial situation and security over time. We need to each create as much value for society as we can through our endeavours and by looking after ourselves and those around us. Individuals and private organisations also need to play a proactive role in fighting inflation by spending and investing wisely.

We have a right to a happy and fulfilling life and to build our wealth, including minimising our tax burden. However, we must be ethical and conscious in our purchasing decisions, as they have far reaching social and environmental impacts. In addition, if lucky enough to have one, we should consider donating a proportion (e.g. 10%) of our financial surplus to charity and good causes to help others, our environment and the communities in which we live. The government needs to create the right conditions for people to do this and provide an adequate safety net when things go wrong or for those who cannot provide for themselves.

The public needs to be educated about money and economics to be more informed and in control of what affects our prosperity and wellbeing. Read as much as you can on Modern Monetary Theory, its advocates and its critics and decide for yourself, as well as reading on economics more widely. If you agree with the overall premise of the theory and this book, then share the information as widely as you can. Contact your local political representative to make them aware of the arguments and literature on the subject. Challenge politicians, your friends, your colleagues and your family when they talk of government expenditure in terms of households and businesses that need to balance the books. This isn't the reality and it hampers our ability to raise our collective prosperity.

As discussed at the start of the book, the cost of inaction and inadequate investment in people, the environment and the economy is significantly greater, and even threatens the existence of civilised society itself. The key to society thriving is the creation of money and its investment in key priorities in a non-inflationary way. I hope that you now have a new perspective on public debt, how money is created and how its power can be harnessed to bring about positive change for society. Government debt and deficits can indefinitely be sustained through money creation and are actually good for society, since expenditure on essential investments also creates equivalent assets for individuals and the private sector. Contraction of public debt through austerity takes away from private wealth and is economically destructive.

By raising general wealth levels and economic growth, you increase the pool of bond buyers available to keep interest payments low on national debt and can ensure that debt falls or is at least maintained as a proportion of GDP over time. There may be emergency periods where public expenditure needs to grow faster than GDP and wealth to head off recessions, deal with disasters and to tackle existential threats like climate change.

However, in the long run you generate new and increasing tax revenues which reduce the need for new borrowing relative to the size of the total economic pie. This creates a virtuous cycle instead of the stagnation we are now facing. With a new perspective on private and public money creation, we can significantly increase the pool of financial resources available to tackle societal issues. This gives us the space to be creative, innovative and generous in potential solutions and approaches to dealing with problems, such as Universal Basic Income and poorer country debt forgiveness.

The success of our human endeavour depends on the public sector, private organisations and individuals all working together and using all the available financial tools at our disposal responsibly. I hope that by reading this book you feel more optimistic about our collective prospects and inspired that something can be done to materially improve our lives over time, by taking actions and investments now.

I have attempted to be succinct and clear in explaining a range of economic concepts for non-economists. Undoubtedly, the limitations of my own understanding and ability to explain, as well as the brevity of each element, have led to some details being simplified and omitted. This detail matters in the practical implementation of the recommendations of this book and MMT. Careful management and planning is needed to ensure they are effective and mitigate any policy risks as much as possible.

However, I believe that the broad arguments of Modern Monetary Theory are self-evidently true. I encourage you to do your own research and find out for yourself the reality of money and government debt and to spread the information far and wide. To repeat the introduction, we can and do deserve better than what our current system is delivering and must become the responsible stewards of our precious and unique planet that we have the potential to be. I hope that you will see that money is no object and society can afford everything it needs to thrive. Let's all act now to make it happen!

Please share and do reach out to discuss the book further. Your reviews on Kindle / Amazon Store are highly appreciated as it helps it reach more people.

Thanks, Dean - @dean_econ

Final Chapter References

[1] Balance of Payments (BOP) Definition, Kenton, 2022 (Investopedia)

About The Author

I am a UK based economist that has nearly ten years of experience in applied economic roles in the public and private sectors. I graduated from Newcastle University in Economics and completed a masters in Environmental Sciences at the University of East Anglia, with an environmental economics specialism.

I am passionate about the pragmatic application of economics to make the world a better place and the communication of the subject in a clear and concise way. I have worked on environmental and climate change policy impact assessments, local authority plans and sustainability opinions. I have done investment appraisal of utility infrastructure spending proposals and estimated the monetary value of social and environmental consequences of programmes and policies.

This book is the first I have written and is purely a personal project. I wrote it because I want to try and make the world a more abundant, resilient and safe place in my own small way. I recently became a father and want to ensure that my daughter has a future that is full of opportunities, where she is safe and free and where there is a stable and healthy environment.

I have often seen great investments, policies and proposals that would have significant social and environmental benefits be rejected on affordability or profitability grounds. However, having learned about the nature of our financial system and that money can be created without limit digitally, it is simply a lack of knowledge and understanding that is holding us back from making the necessary investments for us all to thrive.

I am an optimist by nature and recognise the abundance and technological marvels produced by our economic system, unlike at point in human history. However, we are threatening the natural systems and social cohesion on which we rely, with habitat destruction and the growing extreme inequalities between and within nations. Despite the sometimes overwhelming scale of the issues we face, we do have the power to put ourselves back on a sustainable path that more equally shares the benefits of progress. Through my writing, I wish to share ideas that I think will help society thrive and survive long into the future.

I hope you have enjoyed reading this book.

Thank you for using your precious time to do so,

Dean

Printed in Great Britain
by Amazon

86136120R00078